FOR HIS GLORY

BARBARA GRIFFITH - BOURNE

MINISTRY IN ART PUBLISHING
The Seal of Excellence

Ministry In Art Publishing Ltd
email: publishing@ministryinart.com
website: miapublishing.com

This publication is designed to provide accurate and authoritative information in regard to the subject matter covered.
It is sold with the understanding that the publisher is not engaged in rendering legal, accounting, or other professional service. If legal advice or other expert assistance is required, the services of a competent professional should be sought.

ISBN: 978-0-9560996-7-9

Cover Design: Allan Sealy
www.miadesign.com

Dedication

I lovingly dedicate this book to the honour and glory of my God, the Father of our Lord and Saviour, Jesus Christ who is the source of my inspiration, the centre of my joy, the spring of my peace and fulfilment.

I gratefully give Him thanks and praise for picking me up from the mire of sin when I fell and, for giving me a second chance by his Special Grace, where His plans and purposes for my life could be fulfilled.

CONTENTS

CONTENTS

Foreword

It's an honour to be asked to write the foreword 'For His Glory'! To have a dream is a wonderful thing, to nurture it and to see it fulfiled is an achievement.

This book is an inspiration and a 'must read' with an open mind, one that speaks possibilities; one that says, 'if you discipline yourself and believe in the treasure that's hidden inside of you, it will one day be discovered'.

These are diverse poems of encouragement and hope and throughout which you can hear that 'He' is the source. These are poems for both young and old that will suit most tastes and persuasion – easy to read and understand and which speaks to and of the human experience.

For the Author of 'For His Glory', a new chapter in her destiny is written. If you too believe in your vision, you'll be next!

Rev Dr J M Thomas

Aim of Book

Although the poems are meant for reflection and pleasure, they have a scriptural basis. You will notice that in some of the poems I have lifted some truths from God's precious word and put them in poetic form. For others, I've drawn inspiration from God's wonderful creation, His characteristics or from real life occurrences.

My desire is that all who read or hear these inspirational poems would receive great pleasure and deep joy like I felt when I composed them.

My sincere thanks for allowing me to share with you my revelation of **His** heart!

Acknowledgements

Special thanks to the late Mother Elbertha Griffith and the late Reverend McDonald Griffith, my parents, who dedicated my life to the glory of God and taught me to love the Lord and were very instrumental in focussing my mind heavenward. Peace be unto them.

Special thanks to the late Elizabeth Small, my grand-mother, who influenced my childhood years with Christian principles. (The poem, 'A Virtuous Woman' is dedicated to her memory). Peace be upon her.

Special thanks to Rev Dr J M Thomas, my Pastor. Through his dynamic *motivational* preaching and teachings, including the topics - *'maximising your potential'* and *'harnessing your vision',* I was enthused, stretched and challenged to take the plunge in bringing my vision to fruition. Sincere thanks and appreciation also for his invaluable encouragement and support in the birthing of this book. (Mine is one of the many exciting successes story. There are numerous testimonies of personal accomplishments and new business ventures due to Rev Thomas' faith-filled ministry). May God preserve his Anointing!

Special thanks and appreciation also to Dr Michael Torres whose expository teaching at our church convention on *'Bringing to birth your Gifts and Talents'* has helped to propel me to labour and deliver by God's grace this book – "For His Glory"!

Special thanks and appreciation to my brother, Elvin whose invaluable support, help and encouragement was second to none. I express much gratitude to him also for his help with proof-reading and good advice.

Sincere thanks and appreciation to my spiritual Sister and Friend, Joan Edwards for her invaluable support, PR strategies and encouragement in all aspects of the *'For His Glory'* Vision. Much gratitude also to her for her help with proof-reading.

Sincere thanks and appreciation to my spiritual Sister and Friend, Eudora Greave for her invaluable encouragement, prayers and support, in this vision. (The poem, 'Daughters of God', was inspired just after she had encouraged me to write more poems – Bless you for caring, Eudora!)

Special thanks and appreciation to Elder St. Clair Boyce, my cousin who greatly encourages me spiritual and in producing a book about my life. Just a few months ago in conversation he asks me, 'can't you write a book'? (Here it is cous, - Be blessed!)

Special thanks and appreciation to the Senior Mothers – (Pearson, Brown, Spence, Baker, Boyce, Branker and Gray) of my Church and other brethren who earnestly prayed for and encouraged me. May God richly reward them!

There are **numerous other names** which I could add to this list who have been a source of great support and encouragement to me – *you know who you are*! *May your reward from our Father's hand be great.*

POEMS

My Father's Infinitive Feats!

Did you know that God can fly?
Would I dare tell you a lie?
He did fly upon the wings of the wind
And rode upon a Cherub, He was flying!
This declaration may leave you stunned
But it's the Scriptures I relied upon!

Here are more feats I'll tell you about
And if these excite you, you're free to shout!
He sits upon the circle of the earth,
Fire from his mouth kindles coals to a hearth;
He shakes the earth out of its place;
Would you say, 'this is not the case'?

He makes the deep boil like a pot -
Causing its waters to be very hot!
The heaven he stretched out like a curtain
And spread them as a tent to dwell in;
With scales he weighed the mountains;
As a measure the dust he comprehends!
He treads upon the waves of the sea;
Did I hear you say, 'how could this be'?

He weighed the hills in a balance,
He thunders with the voice of excellence!
His voice divides the flames of fire –
According to his will and desire!
He breaks the cedars with his voice -
The fields of the wood should rejoice!

By his breath frost is given;
He directs the rain to fall from Heaven!
The clouds cover the light at his command
How this is done, can any understand?
These divine infinitive feats
Are so magnificent, no one dare compete!
Whatever your opinion of what I've told you about,
Father God's ways are past finding out!

THE REVERENCE OF TREES!

There is no greater Architect
Or nobleman I ever met,
Who hold such power of skill and design,
To make the trees skip like a hind!

Each tree so intricate and unique,
With such exuberance displayed, though meek;
They bow and flutter with such adoration,
Expressed brand new like the 'day of creation'!

They dance, they curtsey in the wind
From root to branches, leaves and limb,
They pay true homage to Almighty God
'Though always in action but never in word!

To watch them bow with reverence to God
Is a humbling sight as they act in accord;
Their action has made me stop and appreciate
God's display of love for mankind's sake!

It is our God, the King, Creator,
Jesus and the Holy Spirit, the Motivator
Who adorned the trees with grace and beauty,
Born out of love and not of duty!

We too have a right to reciprocate
The love freely given by the 'Great Potentate'
Like the trees we should always bow and worship
The Eternal God, so matchless in love and Kingship!

THE EMOTIONAL GOD!

There's no doubt that the Lord God is real,
Scripture spelt out his attributes in detail!
He's the True and Living God
All others that exist are only fraud!
They are false imitators of the truth
They cannot deliver or provide proof!
Yet, some trust in gods of wood and stone
In whom there's no help or favour shown;
Others put their trust in sinful man
As their god for satisfaction!
But above all there's none like Jehovah
Who demonstrates His **love** and **favour**!
He's the **emotional** 'Father of Mercies'
Who's touched with **feelings** of our infirmities!
He's the God who has no equal
Neither is He comparable!
Kings and nations fear His Name
His **power** and might brought him fame!

He displays His **beauty** in creation
Touching human hearts with spiritual **passion**!
His **eyes** run to and fro throughout the earth,
His **face** beholds the righteous with **mirth**;
His **ears** are opened unto our cry,
A worthy request he will not deny!
With **joy** and **singing** he lifts His **voice**,
With his whole **heart** for His people He'll **rejoice**!
He **speaks** to those who worship an idol
Saying, 'I'm a **jealous** God', so be mindful!
His **kindness** is without condition,
He extends his **mercies** to any generation!

He gives victory and **saves** his people from harm
With His strong **hands** and stretched our **arm**!
His characteristics are very well known
Like **wrath**, **justice** and loving **passion**!
As a giver of gifts He daily gives a present -
The 'Gift of Life' that some may resent
And He, so loved the world that He **gave**
His son that whoever believes shall be saved!

THE VOICE WE CAN'T IGNORE

There is a voice we can't ignore,
Whatever it commands, it is steadfast and sure,
It is the voice of the Lord, Jehovah
Who speaks to his people over and over!

The voice of the Lord moves upon the waters,
It is heard as the God of Glory thunders,
The Voice of the Lord is authorative
Yet, full of majesty so expressive!

The voice of the Lord breaks the cedars,
Even the 'Cedars of Lebanon' that towers!.
He causes them to skip like a calf in the dance,
Lebanon and Sirion like unicorns that prance!

The voice of the Lord divides the flame of fire -
He gives the fire of the Spirit we desire!
The voice of the Lord shakes the wilderness,
The wilderness in the land of Kadesh!

The voice of the Lord makes the hinds to calve
And find the forest where meat they could have;
Everyone speaks of His glory in the temple,
Giving thanks and praise to the fullest!

THE LAW OF LOVE

Our God's Commandments are to be believed
We must obey these principles that are our creed;
It's our duty to observe and keep each commandment
And teach them to our children as an aid to chastisement!

These principles bear our God's love for mankind,
They're not harsh rules to crush us down,
They lovingly express who our God really is
Declaring righteousness and truth that is His!

The 'Law of Love' says there is and should be no other God;
In truth, no one but Him has created this world;
We should not practice any form of idolatry
For to Almighty God this act is contrary!

We should not swear by God or in vain take His Name,
As we are the only ones that will take the blame;
Remember the 'Day of Rest' to keep it holy
And give God his merited honour, praise and glory!

Honour Father and Mother that our days may be long
In the land with the people that we dwell among;
We should not kill or commit adultery,
Robbing someone of life and causing human misery.

We should not steal what is not ours or tell a lie,
Our words should be is honourable on which all can rely!
We should not want or take what is not ours;
Honesty is the best policy and that's the way it goes!

CLOUDS OF LOVE

While high up in the skies on 17/8/03,
I saw my Father's love displayed for me,
It was no ordinary expression of His love
But, 'So Love' was written in the clouds above!

Looking out of the aeroplane,
God's masterpiece enthralled me in the main,
I prayed, 'Father write your love upon a cloud'-
Taking care not to shout aloud!

For words I then sought and looked,
And was prepared to search as long as it took;
I knew that my Father would not let me down
As He's faithful and never does wrong!

I thought I would look for the letter 'L' first,
Followed by 'o', 'v', 'e' or in reverse,
But my Father so omnipotent and true
Had painted 'So Love' in the azure hue!

I first spotted a large letter 'S'
Then followed by 'o' and all the rest,
I realise that God in His wisdom and high esteem
Had confirmed his truth in **St. John 3 v 16**!

My love I give as I readily reciprocate,
His gift of Salvation I do appreciate,
I thank and praise Him for loving me always,
I'll love Him for the rest of my days!

AN INSTRUMENT OF PRAISE

We are the 'Instruments of God's praise',
This is what the Bible says;
Praise Him now, all nations,
Come, praise Him in the congregations!

We should not stand idle or make an excuse
For Instruments are futile when not in use,
Praise is sweet music to God's ears
Each and every time our voice he hears.

If you were likened to a musical instrument
Would it be one from the Old Testament?
Which one would God prefer you to be?
Would it be ancient or contemporary?

The harmonious organ may be his preference,
Combining the notes of the guitar in sequence;
Maybe He might choose you as a violin
With notes like the 'sweet psalmist' harping!

He could like Miriam use you as His Timbrel
Sending out triumphant sounds in Israel!
He could use you to signal as a trumpet,
Or choose you as a resounding Clarinet!

Would you be God's Saxophone?
Or be His Oboe, with a loud and thin tone?
Would He use you like the flute to attract
Lost souls for Jesus and bring them back?

Perhaps, He may use you like the Dulcimer
To awaken Saints from their slumber
So they could sing praises before dawn
And melodious music early in the morn!

Whatever the instrument my Lord may choose,
Be ready and willing as the Holy Spirit moves,
Let Him make you an 'instrument of His praise'
Making sweet melody all your days!

A SON IS A GIFT!

A Son is a gift from God, so dear,
A bundle of joy to cherish and care,
To teach and admonish in all ways of truth
That life should be meaningful in his youth!

Son, 'though some people may disappoint you,
God, the Father is faithful and true!
He sees and knows what causes you pain
And provides needed comfort in Jesus' Name!

Life is for living, giving and sharing;
My son, I beg you, do not forget 'thanksgiving';
It is the main ingredient for a life of success,
As those with money only, would soon confess!

You can be assured that God's love is always new
'Though trials of life may keep it from view;
Some mothers may sometimes forget their son,
But God will remember, for He's the Omnipotent one!

For Neil

The Day I entered a different World

My birth date signified
The moment I first cried!
Dating the first breath I drew
A task for me, very new!
A place in history I claim
A place that will never be the same
It was the start of a new experience
Something of significance!
The comfort of the womb I was forsaking
For challenges that were awakening
I was to take my chance in life
Facing emotional battles and strife,
It was a historical occasion
A day picked out of God's creation!
A mark on the clock of time
A moment so sublime!
New horizons were unfurled
When I entered this different world!

For Hannah

THE SWEET SIXTEEN QUESTIONS

Does 'sweet sixteen' means
That you've awaken from childhood's dream
Controlled by parental discipline
Where your life was all hemmed in?
Does it mean you can stay out very late?
And all chastisement forsake?
Have you escaped parental responsibility?
Because you've experienced mere puberty?
Does it mean you'll shed no more tears?
Having left behind your primary years?
Would you no longer have to be told?
Or even be scold?
Would you not heed instructions?
Given to you for Godly directions?
Do you now know everything?
Thinking you've turned an adult at 16?
Should you not embrace 'wisdom's reproof?
At this remarkable stage of your youth?
Wisdom is more precious than gold
And is relevant for both young and old;
The start of wisdom is to reverence the Lord,
Embracing his truth in accord!
Let wisdom be your special delight,
It will guide and teach you right!

The infallible Word

Remember your Creator the Bible says
And pay special attention to all His ways,
Never lean to your thoughts however demanding,
But trust in the Lord for sound understanding!

Get familiar with the Word and diligently seek
God's divine wisdom so satisfying and unique;
It is the soul food for young and old alike
Who would be filled with this heavenly delight!

Get deeper into the Word for fullness and health
Where abides no earthly kingdom or wealth,
For God's infinite wisdom is all so complete
To wise-hearted people who His promises keep!.

The 'Word' is a weapon of defense, though not carnal
To be used against every trick of the Devil,
So stand upon the precious sword of the 'Word'
For continual victory at home and abroad!

The Youth's Defender

You will find no one kinder
As my Lord, the Youth's Defender;
He is gracious, true and kind
With an ever loving mind.

Some Youths today have gone astray
From the straight and righteous way
But my Lord will not see them lack,
So He will tenderly brings them back!

It is a challenge to keep youths in the fold -
Young people should be brave and bold,
Endeavouring to keep the enemy at bay,
By keeping in step with Jesus night and day!

Young people cannot fight life's battle alone
As Satan has cornered every angle and zone,
But the Youth's Defender is close at hand,
He's the one who is always in command!

There's no need for youths to faint or quit
Since God's armour is divinely made to equip
Soldiers who join the 'Heavenly Brigade'
And is available for the Master's parade!

Indeed, there's a prize and crown to be won
By overcomers when life's work is done
So up, young people, be fearless and strong,
For the 'Youth's Defender' will never let you down!

Time is Precious

Time is precious for all good reasons,
And to everything there are seasons,
A time to every purpose under the heaven,
You need redeem the time that is given!

Take time to pray to the Father each day
Listening carefully to what He has to say;
Praise Him daily for health and strength,
Read and study His word at length!

Take time to thank Him for parents true
Not forgetting to count your blessings anew;
Take time to value the beauty of creation,
Show gratitude and appreciation!

Give thanks daily for the Saviour God sent,
Aspiring to view the place where he went;
Always reflect on your journey each day
Remember to keep close to Him all the way!

Pray before you go

Pray before you get up and go,
And never open your front door
Without first committing your life to God,
Who's given advice to pray in His Word!

You need His protection without and within
If you the battle of life here will win,
Do not be too busy or hurried to stop
For your daily re-filling and spiritual top-up!

The paths unknown may be fraught with danger
For unprotected souls who may stop and linger
Where your 'adversary' throws his evil dart
To pierce an unwise soul through their heart!

Go! get to that sacred inner chamber,
Where the Saviour is waiting, so do not ponder;
Let him cover you in the armour of God;
Your needed protection you can always afford!

For Wendy

The Mighty Wind

The wind is an all powerful force
Though some may deny its origin and source!
Almighty God, like the wind we can't see
Yet, He exists and always will be!

The wind, like all nature God's will obey,
But Humans refuse and say, 'nay, nay'!
Nature's elements cannot their way choose,
They obey and by God's order they move!
He commands and raises the stormy wind
That lifts up the waves that seem unending!

With powerful force the wind will uproot trees
And lay them to rest wherever it may please;
Invisibly it moves objects from place to place,
Hurling them far and wide or up into space!
Sometimes, so ferocious as if by craft
The wind takes and destroys everything in its path;
No one can its actions turn off or turn on,
But just endure its effects until they are gone.

Anyone not wearing a hat or scantily dressed
The wind will uncover or make their hair a mess.
It tosses the leaves and dust all around,
While making a hissing or a screeching sound!

If we could acknowledge the Creator's plan,
Then we'd find it better to understand
That the wind is merely fulfilling His word,
Like the rest of creation is acting in accord!

Mary Magdalene's Easter Phenomenon!

Followers of Jesus thought all hope was lost
As they witnessed that Jesus had died on a cross
But Mary's act of sheer determination
Brought about her Easter phenomenon!
Mary was not one to give up hope;
Her faith in Jesus no adversity could revoke,
The scene at the cross was not the end
For on Jesus' word she could depend!

Mary found Jesus as her precious Pearl
The very best in the entire world!
Could it be that Jesus had now deceived her?
After declaring to be the Messiah!
Could she over accept that the end had come?
Surely, there must be a Resurrection!

Mary's intention was to find her Lord
And take him away, if only by fraud;
Early on Easter morn went Mary Magdalene
Demonstrating faith so rarely seen!
She hastened to the tomb without fear
Although darkness overshadowed her way!
On arrival she found the stone rolled away;
Death could not Jesus' body delay -
Silencing the critics and putting them to shame;
A phenomenon for Mary, Jesus had risen again!

Mary ran in haste to find Simon Peter
And John to bring them to the sepulcher;
She gave them tidings of joy and cheer
That the stone at the tomb was rolled away!
Both disciples ran there to check out the story
For indeed, God alone must get the glory!
Jesus has risen from the dead in truth,
The empty tomb was now full proof!

The two disciples somehow did not tarry
To share the news, they decided to hurry
But Mary, full of faith had determined to wait;
An appearance of Jesus was not too late!

Mary Magdalene's Easter Phenomenon!

So sure of results that Mary stooped down
And, lo and behold, two angels sat around
Where the body of Jesus had lain
All clothed in white and glistening!
Mary turned as Jesus called out her name,
Bringing to birth her universal fame!
She, overwhelmed with a joyous sigh,
Excitedly replied, "Rabonni"!
"Touch me not", Jesus instructed,
"I have not yet to my Father ascended,
But go to my brethren with the news of love
That I ascend to our God and Father above"!

What are you seeking from Jesus today?
Is your expectation familiar or rare?
If you exercise full faith and determination
You like Mary will experience a phenomenon!

THE ROSE GARDEN

Life is not a 'garden of roses',
Struggles may rob you of joy and reposes
Yet, life should be lived one day at a time
Asking the Creator for guidance sublime;
He alone is the Great 'Plan Maker'
With designs and patterns for the taker
Who would humbly ask His will
In their daily life to fill!

Never think, 'I can go it alone'
When the Plan Maker His love has shown -
Although you do not know the whole plan
Or, even fully understand,
No circumstance is beyond his reach,
So never, ever retreat!

Dearest child, remember this,
For peace, satisfaction and bliss
Trust in God's wisdom and might
For that 'Rose Garden' of delight!

For Marisa

Summer Fruits

Summer fruits need the warmth of the sun
For health and vitality to ripen!
Great pleasure they bring to the taste
If they're not developed in haste!
Equally, people need the Holy Spirit's fire
To burn out sin's dross and shape their desire!
The 'fruit of the spirit' mentioned in Galatians five
Will keep the soul healthy and alive!
These fruits of the Spirit are always in season
And are available without condition!
There are nine of these spiritual nutrients
Designed to help us brave life's elements;
There is Love, Joy, Peace, Faith and Patience,
Gentleness, Goodness, Kindness and Temperance!
Indulge yourself in these fruits each day
For strength and courage all along the way!

A Lesson in the Leaves

Autumn leaves stand out in glorious splendour
In luxurious colours, we may sometimes wonder,
Why didn't they remain on the trees
Where they were floating in the breeze!

In rich array of lemon, orange, and brown
They fall in their thousands to the ground,
To indicate that we should learn
A lesson in transience they beckon us to discern!

Like the leaves we begin life, as some say - green
Then, in the Autumn of life some wrinkles are seen;
We may get bigger or become very small,
While others, because of ill-health may slip and fall!

Some folks misconceive that time is forever,
And to accomplish their dreams they may steal or borrow;
They do not realise that like the leaves they will fall,
When death their number has decided to call!

Do not be complacent and take life for granted,
Since we're accountable for the life we have started;
Like the leaves our seasons will come to an end
And we must answer the question, "what then"?

WINTERTIME!

Winter is the coldest season of the year,
Its effect causes much dread and fear!
People often moan and gripe
And complain on a cold winter's night!
Visions of 'winter' are of ice and snow,
Frosty days and chilly winds that blow,
Icy roads and the frozen lake,
Darkened mornings when we awake!
Heaps of snow blanketing the ground,
Turning traffic and travel upside down!
Hearts are filled with trepidation,
The body mode is drawn to hibernation!
Winter may become unbearable
But gratitude is good principle;
In God's word so very bold
He asks, "who can stand against the cold"?

He gives snow like wool,
A treasure rare and beautiful!
He scatters the hoar frost like ashes
Which seizes everything it possesses;
He cast forth ice like morsels,
A picture resembling crystals;
He sends his word and melts them
When they're still frozen!
Praise Him Snow, Hail and Vapour,
Let all things Praise Him for ever!

The Treasures of Winter

Wintertime bring children pleasure
When delightsome snowflakes gather!
This gift is poured upon the land,
A mysterious treasure from the Father's hand!

Freshly fallen the snow is a lovely sight,
When viewed, especially at night;
Oh! the beauty of the snow covered leas,
The glory from God's treasuries!

These luxurious white flakes
Transform the rivers and lakes;
The housetops are carpeted white,
Much to the children's delight;

Treetops bear particles of snow
That glistened in the light and glow,
Each droplet shines like a diamond,
Icy mountains resemble a white kingdom!
The earth is blessed with nourishment
For crops and food for man's content!

A time of Spring

Springtime brings an air of excitement
That makes every heart joyous and expectant!
God crowns the year with his goodness
And all His paths drop fatness!
They drop upon the pastures of the wilderness
And the little hills rejoice at His greatness!
He blesses the earth and waters it,
It is softened with showers when he visits!
Does He not settle the furrows
By making them soft with showers?

The earth awakes from her long rest
And buds shoot forth with beauty and zest!
The birds are heard chirping and singing,
Children in the playground will be skipping,
The bees will be gathering honey
On days that are bright and sunny,
Flowers bloom with magnificence
And the air is perfumed with hyacinth,
Each Daffodil tries to lift its head,
While ducks in the pond look up for bread!
Every living thing their chance have taken
As the forces of nature are awaken
To and embrace the sweet joys of Spring
As the Church bells peal with a welcoming ring!

DAUGHTERS OF GOD

Daughters of God, it's plain to see
That Jesus gave you liberty!
He shattered your shame and scorn,
Lifting you from fear forlorn!
He delivered you from Satan's strife,
Elevating you as a channel of life!
Let your spiritual eyes perceive,
Your master's favourable decrees;
Negative customs may have held you back,
Binding you in a state of lack,
But Jesus in his grace and mercy
Took your burdens and left you free,
Opening doors to possibilities!
He exchanged your ashes for beauty,
Handing you love's golden key!

Shape up now, you daughters of God,
You are his prize and reward –
A rose in his chosen bouquet,
A diamond among many so rare!
The woman's seed bruised Satan's head,
Ridding you of sin and dread;
Use no excuses to stay in the background,
Go forth with confidence abound!
Daughters of God have some tasks to do,
Deborah led an army, so how about you?
Boldly send doubts and regrets on their way,
Embrace with courage your inheritance today!

Jesus showed that women have a place,
One of honour in the human race;
He defied tradition's protocol
To lift you up from Adam's fall;
He appointed Mary a missionary
On purpose to ratify his decree
So women could claim their inheritance
And fulfil their role of significance!
Come out today, from beneath the shadows,
To the amazing future of your tomorrows!

For Eudora

DADDY'S LITTLE GIRL

She knew she was 'daddy's little girl'
And for her, daddy was her world!
Wherever he was, she wanted to be,
Although this was an impossibility!

While at home and walking around the farm
She would run into daddy's strong arms
As some animals made her afraid,
At times she felt very scared!

Whenever daddy went away
She would often kneel and pray
Believing that Daddy God was near
Who would dry her falling tear!

At times she would sob and weep
Until she cried herself to sleep
And look forward to daddy's home-coming
Anticipating the gifts he would be bringing!

Her junior years, especially
Were cherished times of quality;
She and daddy would make and fly kites
And strolled through 'Bridgetown' some nights!

Circumstances caused daddy's girl to move abroad –
Sad separation bears no sweet reward -
Although she and daddy were miles apart,
She knew she was daddy's girl in her heart!

Through ill-health daddy went to the USA
For a rest and a long holiday;
He arranged to meet his little girl on that day,
But the 'plane had a severe delay!

As daddy's plane flew out, hers flew in
On the tarmac it was landing,
So by minutes she missed him –
Never to see him again
As death took him, all the same!

Daddy's Little Girl

In feelings of grief and abandonment
Daddy's little girl wept and lament,
Soon, comfort came as Daddy God spake –
His little girl he did not forsake!

Now for comfort the little girl would run
Into the arms of Daddy God's Son,
Who gave his life to set her free
And the hope that 'daddy' again she'll see!

MUMMY DEAR!

I was not the child you wanted me to be,
Yet, I love you dearly, mummy!
Time and again I was told
How deeply I wounded your soul,
So please forgive my childhood folly,
I didn't quite understand, you see -
That I cause you much headache
When your parental rule I would break;
At times I performed mean tricks
Just for fun or mere kicks;
I would hear you chastise and shout
Then I'd wonder, 'what is this all about'?
I didn't know that I was wearing you down
When I acted like a thoughtless clown!
My crocodile tears did not help
When you threaten, 'I'll get the belt'!
I thought it best to get my own way
And ignore what you would say!
How strange that life has a 'pay day' –
Now my child behaves in the same way!
I hear an echo from my past
When to scolding, my child laughs!

THE ELECT LADY

This title depicts an honour so grand,
Elected by God and not by man!
A Lady of such calibre is in great demand
Her ratings are high, you'll understand?
Her tasks and responsibilities are rarely seen
But her leadership is held in high esteem
Her teachings you may desire to sample
For her conduct is marked by good example!

Is there such a Lady in our Town?
That merits this title so profound?
Is she merely an item of décor?
Would she throw away what she has laboured for?

I now refer to the second Epistle of St. John
Where there are 'Words of Wisdom' to look upon;
Perhaps, John is addressing a Church in particular
Or, an unnamed Lady with whom he's familiar!
A lady of honour and such distinction
Is surely the chosen daughter of Zion -
The Bride of Christ, to be exact
Who is reminded of the virtues she lacked!

St. John, the Elder and Apostle of Love,
Sends greetings from Jesus and the Father above
To the Elect Lady and her children
With Words of Truth he admonished them –
To teach sound doctrine and the truth proclaim
And portray true love in Jesus Name;
He begged them to walk in God's Commandment
Which from the beginning was Heaven sent!

John makes a declaration that tells
Of love in whose heart the truth dwells,
And emphasises the need to be steadfast
For the sake of the truth that will last!
He rejoiced that some stood upon the truth;
Surely, they had received it from their youth!
It was given from God, the Father
Saying that they should love one another!

THE ELECT LADY

John warns of deceivers who had transgressed
By denying that Jesus Christ came in the flesh;
These possessed the spirit of anti-Christ
And bear false witness of the Devil's device!
Those who stood not in the teachings of Christ
Receive them not, or their favour entice,
Neither give them place, nor wish them God's speed,
Do NOT be a partaker of their evil deed!

John concluded - 'Until I see you face to face'
Abide in Love and God's saving Grace
That your joy may be full, again and again,
Your Elect Sister greets you, Amen!

For First Lady, Jemis Thomas

MONTELLE!

A good friend is more precious than gold
And you are that one, let it be told!
You cared and showed me love from the start,
I regarded you my sister, in heart!

Your care and watchful eye for me at school,
Often saved me from the Headmaster's rule;
On my behalf you would answer my name
As my stammer caused me shame!

Although I travelled over hill and dell
Is there a dearer friend than you, Montelle?
You stood out amongst the rest,
You are to me, 'the Best'!

Many happy times we shared,
Bountiful fun and games we played,
Along with Sister Pearline
With her sparkling smile and gleam!

Miles and oceans placed us apart
But prayer united us in heart;
We found assurance in our Father's love
That came from his blessings above!

Your kindness and thoughtfulness I cannot deny,
The calibre of your friendship money cannot buy;
Qualities like yours are seldom seen
In our world, they are few and far between!

When ill-health brought you pain,
I prayed for total healing in Jesus' Name,
I prayed God to renew your strength each day
And forever keep you in his care!

Why were you taken, God alone knows
But Heaven has gained a 'Special Rose'!
You are now with Jesus to be at rest –
Montelle, my friend, you're the Best!

(Dedicated to my childhood friend, Montel)

A Virtuous Woman - ('Mammy', My Granny)

There was a humble woman I once knew
Whose life was full of godly virtue;
She taught righteousness explicitly
To relatives, friends and family;
Trust, love, honour and serve the Lord
Ever believing His written word!

Prayers at Breakfast, Lunch and Supper –
Giving thanks for all things on offer!
If you were ever picked upon or blamed
She'd say, 'give up your right for wrong
Instead of causing a big ding dong'!
Or, 'just leave it up to God"
Who's the Giver of our reward!

Her offspring were expected to read a verse
From the Bible they so often rehearsed;
When they were tucked up in bed for to sleep
Without so much of a sound or a peep,
At midnight or at break of day she would say,
'Wake up and pray; keep that old devil at bay'!

Her home was always spick and span
Although some could never understand
Why she should go to such extremes
But her standards had to be pristine!
To illustrate a lesson in tidiness
That, 'cleanliness was next to godliness'!

Her doors were open to family and strangers alike
For shelter, comfort and refreshing delights;
But, whatever the hour or day no one could ever say,
'I left her house without a word of pray'!
Moreover, her good morals were never in question
When she faced any intricate decision!

If you were feeling lone or sad
Because of some problems you've had
And fears and burdens weighed you down
Until under your sorrows you could drown,
These words of wisdom she would share –
'God don't put on us more than we could bear'!

A Virtuous Woman - ('Mammy', My Granny)

At times she may pass a youth on the way
During the fleeting hours of the day,
Standing idle as if life has no meaning
Or, would be joking, skylarking or scheming,
She would approach the lad with a godly word –
'Young man, give your heart to the Lord'!

She was a woman of prudence and etiquette,
Who believed music is Heaven's best gift, yet!
She would urge you to make music or sing a song,
On cold wintry nights when the hours seem long;
She encouraged good living and attention to health,
Commanding you, 'get a book and educate yourself'!

It was one sad and mournful day
That she was called 'Home' as one might say –
Not at a ripe old age or a month to the day,
But God who knows best for calculation
Has promised her a legacy of Salvation –
A 'Light throughout her generation'!

Should you wish to make her acquaintance?
And desire to seek her with diligence,
Let me invite you to call on her Saviour
Who would be happy to introduce her,
All decked in Robes of bright array
At His all heavenly 'Crowning Day'!

ABIDING!

If you abide in Jesus and His words abide in you,
It is expected you'll obey Him in all that you do;
For no branch can bear fruit of itself,
It needs the Vine to develop in good health!

Be spiritually clean and in the 'Word',
Keeping God's laws in love and accord
That His joy may remain in you to the full,
As Jesus our example, did the Father's will!

Jesus has commanded us to love one another
And show compassion to our poor brother;
Greater love has no man than this,
That Jesus gave his life in sacrifice for us.

Jesus has called us 'friends', not servants -
What an intimate title this statement presents!
Bringing us into his circle
Is by all means, a fantastic miracle!

We need always to remember Jesus' word
That the servant is not greater than his Lord,
If the world has persecuted Him who is true,
They will, without doubt, persecute you!

The Antidote of Forgiveness

Many bear scars that plague their emotion
And look for healing from a physician;
Yet, there's an antidote in forgiveness,
That's applicable when they've trespassed!

However hard it may seem a task
Forgiveness is within our grasp!
It is a powerful medicine
When each other we have forgiven!
If a healthy life you must live
When you pray, you need to forgive!
As the Heavenly Father forgives you,
You're expected others to forgive too!
This is the Law of Heaven –
Forgive and you will be forgiven!

If you leave forgiveness too late
It will stop you at Heaven's gate.
If anyone thinks there's a number
Of times to forgive a brother,
Jesus said, 'seventy times seven'
When he was asked the question;

There's no boundary, I must admit
As forgiveness has no limit!
Be sure you act on forgiveness today
And healing will quickly come your way!

The Gift of Giving

God loves a cheerful giver,
Whose heart is pure and is keen to deliver
The gift of love to those in need,
And who'll recognise that this is a good deed!

It's the Lord's command that we should share,
Since He's the one who looks after our welfare
He said, 'freely you have received -
Freely give' and you'll be blessed indeed!

He appreciates when we give to the poor
Who may perchance come knocking on our door;
We may pass some poor person in the street
Or, be aware of their plight when we meet!

By our gifts of love we give seed to the Sower,
For bread that satisfies in the needful hour
We must not forget to minister to God's Saints
And those who are sick and ready to faint!

There is a blessed promise to those who give
Seeds of love that someone might live,
God has promised a return in good measure,
Pressed down and fully shaken together!

The 'Call' of the 12 Apostles

The call of the Apostles as in Matthew 10
May make us wish we were there back then;
Jesus sent them forth overshadowed by his love
To be wise as serpents and harmless as a dove!

Jesus, in calling to him his 12 Apostles
Empowered them against the works of the devil;
To heal all manner of disease –
Now the names of the Apostles are these:

First Simon, surnamed Peter,
Followed by Andrew, his brother's keeper;
James and John who were of Zebedee,
Then Philip and Bartholomew came along with glee!

Next came Thomas and Matthew the Publican,
Who made haste from the receipt of custom!
Jesus then chose James the son of Alpheus,
Followed by Labaeus, surnamed Thaddaeus!

Afterwards He chose Simon the Canaanite,
And last was Judas Iscariot, the 'parasite'!
They were not to go the way of the Gentiles
Or go into Samaria, not many miles!

These 12 Jesus sent to preach the gospel,
Commanding them to go to the lost sheep of Israel;
To heal the sick, cleanse the leper and raise the dead
Giving what they had freely received, the living bread!

CELEBRATING DIFFERENCE

Celebrating Difference
Should be marked with significance!
It is a profound opportunity
To embrace the blessings of diversity!
A time not to focus on oneself in particular,
Rather to celebrate with all people of colour!
Whatever one's age, race or ability
There's a need to celebrate diversity!
Those that are paraplegic or thalidomide
Let them in courage and confidence abide!
They too have a right to celebrate
And in any event participate!

We're all people of value
And this has been proven to be true!
Everyone has a right to an opinion
There's no place for condescension!
We're all blessed with gifts to contribute
So there's no need to pretend to be astute;
We cannot all look the same,
So please, don't apportion blame
To one's birthplace or ancestry,
Just celebrate the blessings of diversity!

Although we may be very different
Individual uniqueness we present;
Diversity is prevalent and will always be
As it is evident for all to see
That our world is one of variety!

Celebrating difference is a time to eat,
To sing and dance with rhythmic beat;
Bring out 'Fried Chicken', sweet and sour
So there's plenty to devour!
Whet your appetite with 'Irish Stew'
And enormous bowls of 'Fufu',
Indulge yourself with 'Fried Dumplings'
And heaps of mouth watering 'Plantains',
Make room for 'Jollof', 'Rice and Peas'
Complimented by all types of 'Curries',
Give delicious 'Welsh Rarebit' a try
With lashings of 'Cous Cous' piled high;

Celebrating Difference

Don't forget the succulent 'Haggis',
You simply must have this!
Eat any day like an English King –
Have 'Roast Beef' and 'Yorkshire Pudding'!

(Apologies if you're not mentioned
In this limited presentation;
Again, I cannot mention every dish
Despite what everyone might wish),
So let's unite and celebrate 'Difference',
Treating everyone with reverence!

THE CENTURION'S FAITH

A man of great faith was that Centurion
Who heard that Jesus was at Capernaum,
His servant was sick, so he could not delay,
For his servant needed a miracle that very day!

With haste the Centurion sent a message to the Jews
Who could not in any way his request refuse,
A favour of Jesus they dared not dismiss,
He was worthy for whom Jesus should do this!
The Jews approached Jesus on him to rely,
To heal the servant who was ready to die,
So off Jesus went to show his compassion
And perhaps meet the great Centurion!

But the Centurion's faith was beyond compare;
He believed in healing without Jesus being there,
He sent friends to Jesus saying, 'trouble not yourself'
As he believed that the servant had recovered his health!
He said, 'I'm not worthy that you should come under my roof'',
The Centurion knew already that he had the proof -
As he exercised his faith all would be revealed
And Jesus only need say so, and his servant be healed!

Divine Marriage

Marriage is Almighty God's idea
Which He ordained, no matter what sceptics say;
This institution is divinely blessed
So a man and his wife should connect with oneness!
God said, 'it is not good for man to be alone',
So He presented him a wife, 'bone of his bone'-
Together with flesh of his flesh,
She was simply, the very best!

Like the marriage performed in Eden,
Marriage is meant to be bliss and not a burden!
A man should his father and mother leave
And with love to his wife cleave!
When a man and a woman has made a bond,
Their marriage romance is never done!
Listen to what Scripture has to say
And this is not in a round about way -
If you want to keep romance alive
Check out the text in *Proverbs five*;
"Drink water out of your own cistern" -
This is not so hard to discern!

Listen again, to what is admonished –
"Let your wife's love be the one you ravish
Rejoice with the wife of your youth,
That your fountain may be blessed in truth"!
Let her be the one who satisfies your desire
When with passion you burn with fire!
Why should you long for a stranger's embrace
That inevitably will end in disgrace?!

Listen well and listen again
So that the Scriptures would not be blamed ;
Should you seek instruction true?
Check out God's word in Genesis one and two;
If you want to keep your marriage romance alive,
Read what it says in Proverbs chapter five!

SOMETHING FOR THE JOURNEY

On life's transient journey
You may not have much money
For all you need to buy
Yet, God promised your need He'll supply;
So it's best to express some gratitude
For his providence of daily food!

When dark clouds appear depicting rain,
I wish you'll give thanks, all the same;
Should you feel lonesome through the loss of a friend?
Friendship with Jesus, I recommend!
If sickness and pain should come your way,
Trust Jesus for healing when you pray!
Though disappointments may block your dream
And things don't appear to be what they seem,
I wish you wisdom to realise
That some opportunities come in disguise!
Make good the short time you're given,
Bringing meaningful goals into fruition!
There will always be some trying tests
Up the ladder to success!

Should undue weariness slacken your pace,
I wish you inner strength for each challenge you face;
In times of turmoil, I speak peace
And perfect order in your plight release!
I speak to you 'beauty' for ashes,
Reminding you of hope's message!
Let not sadness your emotions employ,
Just anoint yourself with the 'oil of joy'!
Acknowledge God through joy and sorrow,
Put faith in Him who holds tomorrow!

For Richard

Aspects of Fruitfulness

Fruits are good for bodily nutrition
Especially consumed if they're ripen!
As with the temporal
So importantly the spiritual -
We should acquire the 'Fruits of the Spirit'
So our soul could benefit!

There is LOVE – often bitter-sweet,
If correctly applied, it is hard to beat!
By love we show we're Jesus' disciple,
Loving one another like his example!

JOY brings a well needed tonic
To body and soul in any climate!
Jesus says, 'let your joy be full –
If you remain in me, it will be plentiful'!
Spiritually eat His words as a start,
Joy will be the rejoicing of your heart!

PEACE is like the calm of a mountain stream
Flowing gently in sweet serene!
Jesus is our Peace, making us one
Removing the wall of separation!

LONGSUFFERING - we cannot simply hurry
Or give up when we become weary;
This calls for plenty of endurance
And double portions of tolerance!

GENTLENESS does not come cheap
As experiences will teach;
As servants of God we must not strive
But show gentleness to everyone alive!
A soft answer turns anger away
And is preferred any hour of the day!

GOODNESS should always abound in our heart,
Inherent in our new birth from the start;
Goodness cannot come out of an evil heart;
Beware of envy, it is not smart;
It will eat you up like a cancer
When there's no antidote or an answer!

Aspects of Fruitfulness

MEEKNESS shows no self or pride,
Often in humility it will hide,
Being submissive in the face of adversity
Showing lowliness as it beauty!

In FAITH the righteousness of God is revealed
Where by Grace our pardon is sealed;
By acts of Faith we could prove
That commanding the mountain it would move!

TEMPERANCE is an act of self-control,
A test of whether we've reached the goal
To demonstrate self-discipline
And sobriety in our daily living;
We are given this with power
To assist us in temptation's hour!

On this very positive note,
We should endeavour to promote
Indulgence in these Fruits every day
For spiritual vitality along the way;
We should demonstrate aspects of fruitfulness
To obtain a bountiful harvest,
Crops and produce of abundance
Cultivated in fields of excellence!

A Spring of Blessings

If your 'Fast' is acceptable to the Lord
He promised a 'spring of blessings' as reward!
When the fast is what God has chosen,
You cease from sin and lift the heavy burden;
Set free those who are oppressed,
Breaking every yoke and seeking God's best;
Give bread to the hungry soul,
Minister to the needy, young and old,
Then your light shall break forth as the morning
As surely a new day is dawning;
Your health will spring up speedily
Advancing in joy and victory!

DAYS UNKNOWN

Each day is an appointment with destiny unknown
Where emerges success or feelings forlorn.
So prepare and be ready come what may,
While asking Jesus to lead you on your way!

Life's tempest and storms will come and go
And tribulations, no doubt may rock you sore,
Be wise and stand upon the sure foundation,
The truth that will keep you in any temptation!

Do not be as the man who built upon the sand
Whose house the floods could not withstand,
But build yours against all tremor and shock,
Just build upon Christ the 'Solid Rock'!

Set not your affections on things here on earth
Where arises famine, drought and dearth,
But send material of faith to build in the skies
Where at last your rest will be in paradise!

OLD YEAR, NEW YEAR!

What does the New Year Hold?
As the hours and minutes unfold
Will it bring peace and laughter
Or more wars and disaster?
Many people will be sure to declare,
"I don't want a year like last year" -
As their lips quaver with fear!
Others may say, 'New Year, New Rules'
Without even preparing their tools!

Whatever the year we've had
Let us rejoice and be glad
As we give thanks for another year;
Let's us join in the Prophet's prayer-
This is found in Habakkuk three
And in earnest let us agree!
And say with one accord
'Revive your work, O Lord!'
In the midst of the years make known
In your wrath, let your mercies be shown!

As the year begins some will make good progress
While others may not stand the test
And draw back from their resolutions
Without seeking any solutions!
As we set goals we need to pray and plan
So God's will we'll better understand!
Many will be making life-changing decisions
That will impact upon many generations!
Some will sign contracts and clinch deals
At home and far fields;
Others will embark on a new career
While some might shed a tear!

As the world comes to term with the devastation
Which took place in the Indian Ocean,
Questions like these are being asked;
Could not the earthquake be forecast?
Was God in His supreme power
In that frightening and dreaded hour?

OLD YEAR, NEW YEAR!

Were these people not righteous?
Were some of them idolatrous?
Will they seek divine remedy?
Will situations be turned to God's glory?

Year 2005 continued with misery and pain,
Global atrocities occurred again and again,
Storms and floods swept across New Orleans
Unleashing havoc the worse that has been!
Thousands felt the effects of Hurricane 'Katrina'
While Mexico was struck by Hurricane 'Wilma'!
Along came the London bombings in July
When terrorists the law of the land defy
Bringing fear and dread to England's shores –
Suicide bombers were now at our doors!
Oh, Lord! Could we cope with anything more?

Just when earth seemed cautiously sombre
South Asia was shaken in bleak October!
A perilous earthquake shook Pakistan,
One of the deadliest ever known to man!
As folk became troubled and frightened,
They searched for answers and begin to question –
Could this be the beginning of the end?
Is there worse to come, then?
Where is God in these times of crisis and loss?
Truth is, He's the place where he was
When Jesus died on a cross!

Society has told God, 'get out of our lives,
We don't need you, we can survive'!
'We exclude you from our schools,
Who need your heavenly rules'?
Sadly, our world needs a 'Divine remedy'
And healing from 'Calvary's Surgery'!
By all means a spiritual revival
And a heart-changing miracle!

An example of Patience!

You may have heard of the man called Job,
Who was perfect and feared Almighty God
He made sacrifices on his children's behalf
And continued to do this while their feast days last!

The experience of Job is a lesson of trust
That we should learn and it is a must!
We should not lose faith however it may seem
That God is unavailable or cannot be seen!

The Devil may desire to sift you as wheat,
But if God allows it, your enemy you'll defeat!
Trust God like Job and possess your soul,
Your change will come; you'll come forth as gold!

Job lost his substance and his children were dead,
But he held on to his faith through fear and dread,
Job said, 'though he slay me I will yet trust in Him'
My ways before Him I'll yet maintain!

Job declared, 'I know that my Redeemer lives' -
He was sure he would see Him as He is
Standing at the latter days upon the earth'
Who Job would behold with a heart full of mirth!

Through days of languishing Job held on to the end,
And a double portion upon him God did send,
God gave him twice as much as he had before,
Job had stocks in abundance, he couldn't wish for more!.

Bethesda Pool

Have you heard the story of the impotent man?
Who waited by the pool in Bethesda land?
He was waiting by the pool for many a year,
Until the Name of Jesus he did hear!

There were numerous sick and impotent folk
Who needed a miracle to help them walk,
They waited for an angel to trouble the water
With a miracle of healing in the Pool of Bethesda!

Along came Jesus on the Sabbath day
Who the impotent man saw as he lay by the way -
Not long after they began to talk
Jesus said to him, 'rise take up your bed and walk'!

The Jews soon heard of the miracle at the pool,
And accused the Lord Jesus of breaking the rule
But Jesus soon conveyed himself away
Knowing that the Father's will he must obey!

SAMSON'S SECRET

Samson, a Judge and son of Manoah,
His strength was not in arrow or bow;
The secret of his strength was his long hair,
Neither man nor beast did he fear!

He was born a purpose to fulfil,
He was by all means the Lord's anointed!
Alas! He was drawn into the enemies' net
By falling in love with a woman he met!

Delilah, a woman of the Philistine,
Enticed him with tricks so very mean;
A man so strong and of great respect –
Could she ever find out his secret?

She seemed to know how to win his heart,
Emotionally, she almost tore it apart –
Delilah laboured night and day
Until Samson gave in to her way!

Samson's secret he should have kept
But he revealed it with much regret,
Thus, he realised that love was untrue
When death came, it was too late to review!

The Runaway Dream!

You woke with an exciting dream
That you were a rich and Royal Queen
Owning the finest diamond ever seen!
As you opened your eyes, it was gone –
Vanished in thin air that very morn!
Trying not to be alarmed,
You applied the rules of calm;
What a mysterious case?
Your dream vanished without trace!
Your Diamond you could not find –
You then started to repine!

In your quest to recapture your dream
You took the path across the stream –
Down the valley, up the hill,
Thinking, you might catch it standing still!
This dream, you must pursue,
You think that it is your due!

You glimpse a distant mountain
Where at the foot lies a fountain –
Your Diamond could be amongst the ripple
Disguised as a frothy bubble,
Flowing along the river ...
Could your dream be lost forever?

At last, there's a flicker of light in the skies;
Would you be deceived by your very eyes?
You see a sparkle from afar -
Oh no, it is only a star!
You urge your dream into fruition,
Yet it hurries into oblivion!

You thought, 'who needs obscurity
When there is colourful notoriety'?
Perhaps, you were fooled by your dream -
Could your thoughts be so mean?
As to tease your emotions at best
In a joke of make-believe, suggest
That you had left poverty behind,
As visions of grandeur cloud your mind?

THE RUNAWAY DREAM!

Maybe the dream lay somewhere
In a place very rare –
You must do what you ought,
Perhaps, you should get a garden fork
And dig deep in the murky earth
For whatever it is worth -
As if for hidden treasure
To realise your heart's desire!

Suddenly, you're overwhelmed with this notion –
Maybe the diamond lies at the bottom of the ocean;
Should you embark on a nautical mission?
In your quest to fulfil your dream
You thought on a plan supreme!
To accelerate your solitary action,
You'll take a speed boat across the ocean;
You'll peer into the water and make a wish -
Your 'diamond' could be in the mouth of a fish!
But, this was to no avail,
You thought, *'I had better get real'*!
You've now exhausted every avenue, it seemed
But still, you chase this runaway dream!
Alas! You thought the quest was in vain,
But you confessed the fact that remains –
'Godliness with contentment is great gain'!

(A scenario that ends in truth!)

THE EXIT QUESTION

Humans make their entrance in this world of sin,
Whether by twos or tens, they're ushered in!
They boldly take their chance
In life's appointment at first glance!
Some enter more briefly than others
Without receiving any flowers!
People come and people go
Some we didn't get to know!
Yet, it is not how we begin
But, if we finish to win!

Everyone has a contribution to make,
However small or great;
It could be a smile you wear,
Or some sentiments to convey;
Perhaps it's a gift you could share.
This way we pass once only,
To make good use of our time is our duty!
Life prevents any rehearsal,
It urges, 'come now and be full'!

How then, will you make your exit?
Will your world indeed benefit?
Will you leave some type of mark
When from life's stage you disembark?
Will you receive an accolade
For some achievements made?
Will your obituary tell of your fame
Or how you've acquired some good name?
On life's stage will you leave an impression
Where you've made a contribution?
Will you carry a beacon or an ensign
When you cross the finish line?
Will you EXIT with a bow?
Ending life's performance, somehow?

THE LIVING "WORD"

Who is the Living **Word**? Some people may ask
And a detailed account may present a great task;
How may the Living **Word** be summarised
Or, be even categorised?

The Living Word is Active Power and Spirit,
The Person of the **Word** Incarnate!
'Word' is termed 'Logos',
With Truth its focal ethos!
Logos declares Christ eternity,
Most absolutely, His Deity!
We can trust **Word's** authenticity
As binding Divine Authority;
We're governed by **Word's** fundamental principles,
That impacts the Holy Oracles!
Word reveals God's purposes for man
Which He desires him to understand!
The Living **Word** is God's revelation,
The Manifested Agent at Creation
When he spoke in the beginning
And life sprung into being!

The Living Word is infallible,
For every circumstance it is suitable;
Everyone could benefit from **Word** Scripture
For free refreshment and nurture;
Mankind are favoured with access rights
To savour the Living **Word** delights!
We can never get enough of this soul food
Or discover its depth and magnitude,
But what we've read and learned we accept
And endeavour not to forget!

The Living **Word** is fresh and ever current,
Always timely and inerrant!
You may say **Word** is suitably versatile,
His effect covers inch and mile!
Word is perfect for navigation,
For the Physician it is the healing medication!
Word warns sinners of Hell and destruction,
Exposing sin and points the way to Salvation;

The Living "Word"

Word is the Christian's Manual and the traveller's map,
Believe it for protection if under attack!
Word is good for reproof and correction,
Profitable for righteous instruction!

See Word's activity from the given theme,
That depicts a '**Word** Tree' supreme –
The Living **Word**-power a seed Creates
And fallen on good ground germinates,
Creating an entrance for the light,
Transforms blindness into sight!
Nurtured by the Spirit **Word** motivates
The soil of the heart generates,
Bringing changes, renewing the mind,
And encourages growth sublime,
Empowering the Spirit with the Anointing that heals
And delivers the soul to fruitful yields!

The Living **Word** features in the 'Beginning',
In the 'End' He sits on a horse, says Rev. 19 v 13;
However we regard Him - first, second or third,
Christ Jesus is THE LIVING WORD!

In gratitude, Dear Father!

Thank you for poetic inspiration
That gives me divine elevation!
I appreciate this special gift
With gratitude and thankfulness!
Thank you for vision and insight,
To pen these words is such a delight!
You stood by me every step of the way,
Urging me on to show that you care;
Thank you for your anointing and bliss;
This experience I could not resist!
You're the only God and Father I know –
I'll magnify your name here below!
Everything I need you will provide
For shelter in your pavilion I hide,
You're my Shepherd, who leads me on,
You'll be there when life's days are done!

HE DESERVES THE GLORY!

Give glory unto the Lord all you mighty,
Praise Him, for it is your duty!
Give unto the Lord the glory He deserves
Worship in holiness and Him only serve!

Give honour and glory with heart and voice,
With reverence and thanksgiving, rejoice!
Sing and dance with heavenly rhythm
Although you may attract criticism!

Make a joyful noise unto the Lord all lands,
Serve Him with gladness and lift up holy hands
Come before His presence with singing
For He is our God from the beginning!

It is He that has made us and not we ourselves
We are his people; we belong to no one else!
Like sheep we dwell in His green pasture,
And rely on Him for comfort and nurture.

Come now, enter His house with thanksgiving
And praise Him for His mercies everlasting!
For the Lord is good and worthy of all glory,
His truth endures to all generations - surely!

FOR HIS GLORY!

As I went to bed one night
With a desire and a mind to write
Poems of inspiration rarely seen
Words of wisdom pure and clean;
I did not know just how to start
But as I prayed words came to my heart;
These poems I dedicate for His Glory
The Omnipotent One and Most Holy!

LaVergne, TN USA
26 October 2009
1608LVUK00001B